To Paula

from M

First published in Great Britain in 1996 by Brockhampton Press, a member of the Hodder Headline Group, 20 Bloomsbury Street, London WC1B 3QA.

This series of little gift books was made by Frances Banfield, Kate Brown, Laurel Clark, Penny Clarke, Clive Collins, Melanie Cumming, Nick Diggory, Deborah Gill, David Goodman, Douglas Hall, Maureen Hill, Nick Hutchison, John Hybert, Kate Hybert, Douglas Ingram, Simon London, Patrick McCreeth, Morse Modaberi, Tara Neill, Anne Newman, Grant Oliver, Michelle Rogers, Nigel Soper, Karen Sullivan and Nick Wells.

Compilation and selection copyright © 1996 Brockhampton Press.

ISBN 1 86019 445 1

A copy of the CIP data is available from the British Library upon request.

Produced for Brockhampton Press by Flame Tree Publishing, a part of The Foundry Creative Media Company Limited, The Long House, Antrobus Road, Chiswick W4 5HY.

Printed and bound in Italy by L.E.G.O. Spa.

Just For You

FRIEND

Illustrated by

Douglas Hall

A.R.C.A.

Selected by Anne Rose

BROCKHAMPTON PRESS

Each day be joy to you,
No day be sad to you,
Honour and tenderness.
Celtic blessing

Look where we will, some human heart has been
Before us with its offering; not a tree
Sprinkles these little pastures, but the same
Hath furnished matter, for a thought, perchance
To some one as a familiar friend.
William Wordsworth, *Home at Grasmere*

True friendship is a union of two fully-formed
personalities, and of the deepest and most inward
part of those personalities ...
Bernard Levin, *Enthusiasms*

A friend is someone who likes you
It can be a boy ...
It can be a girl ...
Or a cat ... or a dog ...
Or even a white mouse.
Joan Walsh Anglund, *A Friend Is Someone Who Likes You*

There are friends that one hath to his own hurt;
But there is a friend that sticketh closer than a
brother.
Proverbs, XVIII:24

The language of friendship is not words
but meanings.
Henry David Thoreau

A man without friends
is like a left hand
without a right.
Ibn Gabirol, *Choice of Pearls*

Have we not been from childhood friends?
Have I not loved thee long?
As long as thou hast loved the night
Whose silence wakes my song.
Emily Brontë, *The Night-Wind*

In the world of relationships, possibly the most
complicated, uncommon, hard to find, hard to
keep, and most rewarding has got to be friendship.
Lauren Bacall, *Now*

Friends are true twins in soul; they sympathize
in everything.
William Penn

These are my friends whose lives were undivided;
So let their memory be, now they have glided
Under the grave; let not their bones be parted,
For their two hearts in life were single-hearted.
Percy Bysshe Shelley, *Epitaph*

Jack Benny was my closest friend in the world.
And of all the great qualities he had, and there
were so many, there was one thing that set him
apart from everybody else. He really thought I
was funny.
George Burns, *All My Best Friends*

A faithful friend is the medicine of life.
Ecclesiasticus, VI:16

There are all kinds of men
 Who have done me good turns,
That I still never think about
 Not for a minute;
Yet if I were making up
 That sort of grace,
They would all of them have
 To be in it.

Rodney Bennett, *A Thank You for Friends*

And, friends, dear friends, — when it shall be
That this low breath is gone from me,
And round my bier ye come to weep,
Let One, most loving of you all,
Say, 'Not a tear must o'er her fall;
He giveth His belovèd, sleep.'

Elizabeth Barrett Browning

If I had to choose between betraying my country and betraying my friend, I hope I should have the guts to betray my country.
E. M. Forster

Friendship is honey — but don't eat it all.
Moroccan proverb

Friendship, on the other hand, serves a great host of different purposes all at the same time.
In whatever direction you turn, it still remains yours. No barrier can shut it out. It can never be untimely; it can never be in the way.
We need friendship all the time, just as much as we need the proverbial prime necessities of life, fire and water.
Cicero

The truth is friendship is to me every bit as sacred and eternal as marriage.
Katherine Mansfield

Love is blind; friendship closes its eyes.
Proverb

Sliding down the banisters,
The day it rained all day,
We played at swings and switchbacks
Like they have Olympia way.
Then folks came in, all wet and cross,
And made us stop our play.
But oh, we did enjoy ourselves
The day it rained all day.
Margaret E. Gibbs, *On the Banisters*

A friend may well be reckoned the masterpiece
of nature.

Ralph Waldo Emerson

◈

Alas, have I not pain enough, my friend,
Upon whose breast a fiercer gripe doth tire
Than did on him who first stole down the fire,
While Love on me doth all his quiver spend —
But with your rhubarb words ye must contend,
To grieve me worse, in saying that Desire
Doth plunge my well-form'd soul even in the mire
Of sinful thoughts, which do in ruin end.
If that be sin which doth the manners frame,
Well staid with truth in word and faith of deed,
Ready of wit, and fearing nought but shame;
If that be sin, which in fix'd hearts doth breed
A loathing of all loose unchastity,
Then love is sin, and let me sinful be.

William Shakespeare, *Sonnets*

18

A hedge between keeps friendship green.
Proverb

There's nothing worth the wear of winning
But laughter and the love of friends.
Hilaire Belloc, *Dedicatory Ode*

A real friend never gets in your way. Unless you
happen to be on the way down.
Anonymous

Happy is the house that shelters a friend.
Ralph Waldo Emerson

Those my friendships most obtain,
Who prize their duty more than gain;
Soft flow the hours whene'er we meet,
And conscious virtue is our treat;
Our harmless breasts no envy know,
And hence we fear no secret foe.

Nathaniel Cotton, *Contentment*

I don't like to
commit myself
about heaven and
hell. You see, I have
friends in both places.
Mark Twain

The truth that is suppressed by friends is
the readiest weapon of the enemy.
Robert Louis Stevenson

Love comes from blindness
Friendship comes from knowledge.
Comte de Bussey-Rabutin

For what do my friends stand? Not for the clever things they say: I do not remember them half an hour after they are spoken. It is always the unspoken, the unconscious, which is their reality to me.

Mark Rutherford

Happiness seems made to be shared.

Jean Racine

Hold a true friend with both hands.

Nigerian proverb

To keep a lamp burning, we have to keep putting oil in it.

Mother Teresa

Be comely and decent in all thy array,
Not wantonly given to sport and to play;
But labour by virtue, in youth, to obtain
The love of thy betters, their friendship
to gain.

Anonymous

In every friend we lose a part of
ourselves, and the best part.

Alexander Pope

My candle burns at both ends;
It will not last the night;
But ah, my foes, and oh my friends —
It gives a lovely light.
Edna St Vincent Millay

Friends part
forever — wild geese
lost in cloud.
Basho, *Haiku*

My brother Jonathan, very pleasant thou hast
been unto me. Thy love to me was wonderful,
passing the love of women.

Samuel II, 1:26

Ah, how good it feels! The hand of an old friend.

Henry Wadsworth Longfellow

When we were little, wandering boys,
And every hill was blue and high,
On ballad ways and martial joys
We fed our fancies, you and I.
With Bruce we crouched in bracken shade,
With Douglas charged the Paynim foes,
And oft in moorland noons I played
Colkitto to your grave Montrose.

John Buchan, *Fratri Dilectissimo*

The only way to have a friend is to be one.
Ralph Waldo Emerson

    And yours is a devotion
that does not bend or alter —
just as the Antarctic Pole
stands opposite the North Star,
   and neither moves,
   your love and my love
shall be steadfast in their loyalty
   and never drift apart.
German poem, early 13th-century

To love is the great amulet that makes this world a
garden.
Robert Louis Stevenson

Love is like the wild rose-briar;
Friendship like the holly tree.
The holly is dark when the rose-briar blooms,
But which will bloom most constantly?
Emily Brontë

The best creed we can have is charity toward the creeds of others.
Josh Billings

Friendship means no separate heart.
Hugh and Gayle Prather

The good neighbour looks beyond the external accident and discerns those inner qualities that make all men human and therefore brothers.
Martin Luther King, Jr

Friendship is the only cement that will ever hold the world together.
Woodrow Wilson

I was angry with my friend:
I told my wrath, my wrath did end.

William Blake, *A Poison Tree*

What is a friend? A single sole dwelling in
two bodies.

Aristotle, *Doigenes Laertius*

Learn to share your friends with other people.
If they're friends worth having, and if *you* are a
friend worth having, they and you will be all the
closer for it.

Elinor M. Brent-Dyer, *Nesta Steps Out*

Be courteous to all, but intimate with few,
and let those few be well tried before you give
them your confidence. True friendship is
a plant of slow growth, and must undergo,
and withstand, the shocks of adversity before it is
entitled to the appellation.
George Washington

Instead of loving your enemies, treat your friends
a little better.
E.W. Howe

True Happiness
Consists not in the multitude of friends,
but in the worth and choice.
Ben Johnson, *Cynthia's Revels*

Besides, he was a likeable man: sweet tempered,
ready witted, frank, without grins of suppressed
bitterness or other conversational flavours which
make half of us an affliction to our friends.
George Eliot, *Middlemarch*

My first, is valued more than gold,
Because 'tis seldom found;
Many there be the name that hold,
With whom 'tis nought but sound.
My second skims the swelling flood
And noble is its air:
It oft has witness'd sights of blood,
And moments of despair.
My third, 'mid life's distressing cares,
A solace sweet and kind;
Happy who call the blessing theirs:
But few that solace find.

The New Sphinx, *A Riddle on Friendship*

I no doubt deserve my enemies but I don't believe
I deserve my friends.
Walt Whitman

This dog and man at first were friends;
But when a pique began,
The dog, to gain some private ends,
Went mad and bit the man.
Oliver Goldsmith, *Elegy on the Death of a Mad Dog*

Always we'd have the new friend meet the old
And we are hurt if either friend seem cold.
W. B. Yeats, *In Memory of Major Robert Gregory*

Thy sting is not so sharp
As a friend remembered not.
William Shakespeare, *As You Like It*

My friends, do they now and then send
A wish or a thought after me?
O tell me I yet have a friend,
Though a friend I am never to see.
Alexander Selkirk, *Monarch of All That I Survey*

That man to man, the warld o'er,
Shall brothers be for a' that.
Robert Burns, *A Man's a Man for a' That*

A friendly eye could never see such faults.
William Shakespeare, *Julius Caesar*

A fav'rite has no friend!
Thomas Gray, *Ode on the Death of a Favourite Cat*

The best of men and friends! we will create
A genuine summer in each other's breasts.
Richard Lovelace, *The Grasshopper: To My Noble Friend, Charles Cotton*

Who's your fat friend?
Beau Brummel, referring to The Prince of Wales

To be honest, to be kind ... and to
spend a little less, to make upon
the whole a family happier for
his presence, to renounce
when that shall be necessary
and not to be embittered, to keep
a few friends but these without
capitulation – above all, on the
same grim condition, to keep
fortitude and delicacy.

Robert Louis Stevenson, *A Christmas Sermon*

Your name may flaunt a titled trail,
Proud as a cockerel's rainbow;
And mine as brief appendix wear
As Tam O'Shanter's luckless mare;
To-day, old friend, remember still
That I am Joe and you are Bill.

Oliver Wendell Holmes, *Bill and Joe*

Friendship is a sheltering tree;
O! the joys that came down shower-like,
Of Friendship, Love and Liberty,
  Ere I was old!

Samuel Taylor Coleridge, *Youth and Age*

Come, let us pity those who are better off
than we are.
Come, my friend and remember that the
rich have butlers and no friends,
And we have friends and no butlers.

Ezra Pound, *The Garret*

I love everything that's old; old friends, old times, old manners, old books, old wine.

Oliver Goldsmith, *She Stoops To Conquer*

It is better to be faithful than famous.

Theodore Roosevelt

Money isn't the only thing you lose the good of if you try to keep it to yourself, and gain by using it. I believe friendship's another. If you share your friends with other people, you risk losing them, of course; but if they're friends worth having you may make them more yours than ever.

Elsie J. Oxenham, *The School Torment*

Friendship in deed was written, not in words:
And with the heart, not pen.
Ben Johnson, *To the Immortal Memory and Friendship of That Noble Pair, Sir Lucius Cary and Sir Henry Morison*

To like and dislike the same things, that is indeed true friendship.
Sallust, *Catiline*

The plague had deprived us all of the capacity for love and even for friendship. For love must have some future, and for us there were only moments.
Albert Camus, *The Plague*

Old friends are best.
King James used to call
for his old shoes;
for they were easiest on
his feet.

John Selden,
Table Talk: Friends

The death of Nelson was felt in England as
something more than a public calamity; men
started at the intelligence, and turned pale, as if
they had heard of the loss of a dear friend.
Robert Southey, *The Life of Nelson*

Choose an author as you choose a friend.
Earl of Roscommon, *Essay on Translated Verse*

My dearly loved friend, how oft have we
In winter's evenings (meaning to be free)
To some well-chosen place used to retire,
And there with moderate meat, and wine,
and fire,
Have we passed the hours contentedly with chat.
Michael Drayton, *First Steps up Parnassus*

To know not faith, nor love, nor law; to be
Omnipotent friendless is to reign.
Percy Bysshe Shelley, *Prometheus Unbound*

When friends fail, and Princes frown,
Virtue is the roughest way,
But proves at night a bed of down.
Sir Henry Wotton,
*The Sudden Restraint of the Earl of
Somerset, Then Falling From
Favour, 1615*

Good thoughts his only friends,
His wealth a well-spent age,
The earth his sober inn
And quiet pilgrimage.
Thomas Campion, *Integer Vitae*

I cannot forgive my friends for dying: I do not find
these vanishing acts of theirs at all amusing.
Logan Pearsall Smith, *All Trivia*

He was my friend, the truest friend on earth;
A strong and mighty influence joined our birth.
Nor did we envy the most sounding name
By friendship given of old to Fame.
Abraham Cowley, *On the Death of Mr William Harvey*

Every time I paint a portrait
I lose a friend.
Attributed to John Singer Sargent

Was it a friend or foe that spread these lies?
Nay, who but infants question in such wise?
'Twas one of my most intimate enemies.
Dante Gabriel Rossetti, *Fragment*

And laughter learnt of friends; and gentleness
In hearts at peace, under an English heaven.
Rupert Brooke, *The Soldier*

In all distresses of our friends,
We first consult our private ends;
While nature, kindly bent to ease us,
Points out some circumstance to please us.
Jonathan Swift, *Verses on the Death of Dr Swift*

I breathed a song into the air,
It fell to earth I knew not where; ...
And the song, from beginning to end,
I found again in the heart of a friend.
Henry Wadsworth Longfellow, *The Arrow and the Song*

In friendship false, implacable in hate,
Resolved to ruin or to rule the state.
John Dryden, *Absalom and Achitophel*

The holy passion of Friendship is of so sweet and steady and loyal and enduring a nature that it will last through a whole lifetime, if not asked to lend money.
Mark Twain, *Pudd'nhead Wilson's Calender*

'Do you come to the play without knowing what it is?' 'Oh, yes, sir, yes, very frequently. I have no time to read play-bills. One merely comes to meet one's friends, and show that one's alive.'
Fanny Burney, *Evelina*

Madam, I have been looking for a person
who disliked gravy all my life;
let us swear eternal friendship.
Lady Holland, *Memoirs*, quoting Sydney Smith

I am the enemy you killed, my friend.
Wilfred Owen, *Strange Meeting*

My wife and I — we're *pals*. Marriage is *fun*.
Yes: two can live as stupidly as one.
Philip Larkin, *Marriage*,

We cherish our friends not for their ability to
amuse us, but for our ability to amuse them.
Evelyn Waugh

A man, Sir, should keep his friendship
in constant repair.
Samuel Johnson

Amathea, most beautiful of cats, why have you
deigned to single me out for so much favour? Did
you recognize in me a friend to all that breathes?
Hilaire Belloc, *A Conversation with a Cat*

Yet I will but say what mere friends say,
Or only a thought stronger;
I will hold your hand as long as all may,
Or so very little longer!
Robert Browning, *The Lost Mistress*

O long, long may the record run,
And you enjoy until it ends,
The four best gifts beneath the sun;
Love, peace and health, and honest friends.
Attributed to Rudyard Kipling, *The Cave Man's Prayer*

The first time I read an excellent book, it is to me
as if I had gained a new friend: when I read a
book I have perused before, it resembles the
meeting with an old one.
Oliver Goldsmith

And if a man lived in obscurity
making his friends in that obscurity
obscurity is not uninteresting.

Yvgeny Yevtushenko, *People*

'Oh, it's Hynde Horn fair,
and it's Hynde Horn free;
Oh, where were you born,
and in what countrie?'
'In a fair distant countrie I was born;
But of home and friends
I am quite forlorn.'

Anonymous, *Hynde Horn*

Friends who set forth at our side,
Falter, are lost in the storm,
We, we only are left.
Matthew Arnold, *Rugby Chapel*

It was a grief to be a friend
Yet to be dumb; to offer peace
And bring the soldiers out ...
Clifford Dyment, *The Encounter*

Acknowledgements:

The Publishers wish to thank everyone who gave permission to reproduce the quotes in this book. Every effort has been made to contact the copyright holders, but in the event that an oversight has occurred, the publishers would be delighted to rectify any omissions in future editions of this book. Children's quotes printed courtesy of Herne Hill School, Hannah Rough and Kingfisher County Primary School; *Of Major Robert Gregory*, W. B. Yeats, from *Collected Poems*, 1912, Macmillan Publishing Co., reprinted courtesy of Macmillan Publishing Co. and A.P. Watt Limited, London; *The Garret*, Ezra Pound, reprinted courtesy of the author's estate; *The Soldier,* from the *Collected Poems of Rupert Brooke*, reprinted courtesy of Sidgwick & Jackson Ltd, a division of PanMacmillan; Rudyard Kipling, from *The Cave Man's Prayer*, published by Macmillan Publishing Co. and Oxford University Press.